NATURE
WALK

The Coyote

NATURE WALK

The Coyote

James V. Bradley

CHELSEA
CLUBHOUSE
An Imprint of Chelsea House Publishers

Chelsea Clubhouse
An imprint of Infobase Publishing
132 West 31st Street
New York NY 10001

Library of Congress Cataloging-in-Publication Data

Bradley, James V. (James Vincent), 1931–
  The coyote / James V. Bradley.
      p. cm. — (Nature walk)
  Includes bibliographical references and index.
  ISBN 0-7910-9114-7 (hardcover)
  1. Coyote—Juvenile literature. I. Title. II. Series: Bradley,
James V. (James Vincent), 1931– Nature walk.
  QL737.C22B63 2006
  599.77'25—dc22   2006011766

Chelsea House books are available at special discounts when purchased
in bulk quantities for businesses, associations, institutions, or sales
promotions. Please call our Special Sales Department in New York at
(212) 967-8800 or (800) 322-8755.

You can find Chelsea House on the World Wide Web at
http://www.chelseahouse.com

TEXT AND COVER DESIGN by Takeshi Takahashi
ILLUSTRATIONS by William Bradley
SERIES EDITOR Tara Koellhoffer

Printed in the United States of America

BANG PKG 10 9 8 7 6 5 4 3 2 1

This book is printed on acid-free paper.

All links and Web addresses were checked and verified to be correct at the time of publication. Because of the dynamic nature of the Web, some addresses and links may have
changed since publication and may no longer be valid.

TABLE OF CONTENTS

Chapter 1

Introduction to the Coyote

AT FIRST GLANCE, A COYOTE looks much like a dog, but if you're lucky enough to get a good look, you will see that the coyote is something different. Its body is high off the ground because of its long, slender legs, and it has a long narrow **muzzle**. It moves more gracefully than a dog. When it trots, the coyote's grayish-tan, lean body and its bushy tail seems to glide over the ground.

The coyote's eyes are yellow, and like all canines, coyotes cannot see color. Sight is the most important sense used in hunting prey, but the sense of smell also plays a

A coyote looks a lot like a dog, but has long, slender legs.

role in hunting and in the coyote's social life. The coyote's ears are erect, long, movable, and pointed, and hearing is excellent.

The coyote's long legs are good for hunting and running after prey on the prairies where many coyotes live. The two long bones of the leg—the radius and ulna—are fused together, as are the bones of the ankle. This prevents the bones from rotating when the coyote twists and turns as it chases its prey. The coyote's fifth toe, called the dewclaw, is located high on its front leg. On the ancient ancestors of coyotes and other members of the dog family, this toe touched the ground. Today, it is sometimes used for eating. Watch how your own dog uses the dewclaw to help turn over large bones.

Coyotes can run for hours without getting tired and can charge up to 40 miles (64 km) per hour in short bursts of speed. Their lung capacity and muscle

COYOTE STATISTICS

Weight: 15–45 lbs (6.8–20.4 kg)
Length with tail: 40–60 inches (1.0–1.5 m)
Shoulder height: 15–20 inches (38–51 cm)
Mating season: January–March
Lifespan: 15 years in the wild
Typical diet: Small mammals, insects, reptiles, fruit, carrion

power have been finely developed to give them great stamina.

The coyote, like the wolf, has lived close to humans since people first settled in North America. Unlike the wolf, however, coyotes have never been tamed. They remain wild and survive—even thrive— in an environment that has been shaped and controlled by humans. They are highly intelligent and highly adaptive members of the wild dog family.

Classifying Coyotes

Some scientists count up to 19 subspecies, or varieties, of coyotes in North and Central America. The color and size of the different varieties are determined by **natural selection**. In desert regions, coyotes are light in color and small in size, while coyotes in the forests and mountainous regions of the northeastern United States have darker colors and a larger size. A coyote in Arizona may be tan or reddish brown and measure 4.5 feet (1.4 m) from the head to the tip of the tail. A coyote in Maine may be blackish-brown and measure 6 feet (1.8 m) in length. All kinds of coyotes have a soft, dense undercoat that is covered by long, coarse, black-tipped guard hairs.

Coyotes belong to the family Canidae, which also includes gray wolves, African wild dogs, Tibetan wolves, and Arctic and red foxes. All together, there are 35 species of **canids** (dog-like mammals) around the world. All 35 species have a common ancestor that lived around 35 million years ago in North America. Coyotes appeared some 2 million years ago and have survived to the present day, even though many of its contemporaries, such as the dire wolf, saber-toothed tiger, and wooly mammoth, went extinct.

HOW COYOTES ARE CLASSIFIED

Class: Mammalia
Order: Carnivora
Family: Canidae
Genus: Canis
Species: latrans

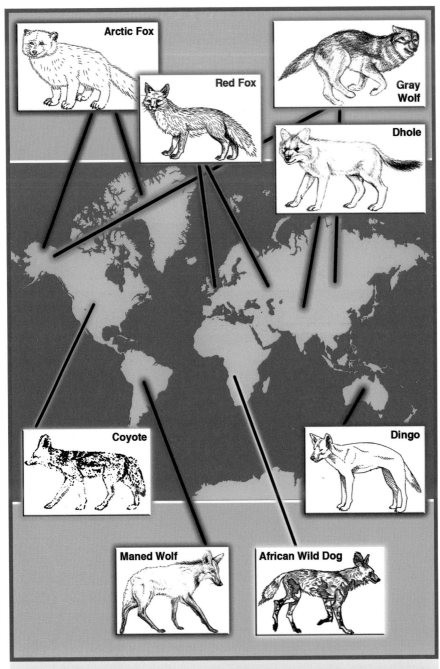

Coyotes are part of the Canidae family. Some of the other species of wild dogs and the places they live are seen on this map.

Studies of fossils show that 2 million years ago, two different populations of canids were well established—the vulpine group and the lupine group. The vulpine group eventually became foxes. The lupine lineage gave rise to coyotes and wolves. Coyotes are true North American canines, having evolved on this continent, and found nowhere else.

Approximately 1 million years ago, coyotes and wolves became separate animals. The **evolution** of both coyotes and wolves was influenced by the Ice Age, which started about 1.5 million years ago and ended about 12,000 years ago. The Ice Age involved four periods when glaciers moved over much of Canada and the northern United States. Each movement of the glaciers was followed by a warmer period when the ice moved back. Both coyotes and wolves adapted to these drastic changes in their environment. The coyotes of the Ice Age looked very much like coyotes look today. They were then, as they are now, predators and **scavengers** that lived on the fringes rather than being a dominant animal in the **food chain**. Their lifestyle worked for them. While other Ice Age mammals became extinct, the coyotes survived.

Coyote Distribution

The coyote's original territory mainly included the grasslands west of the Mississippi River from the

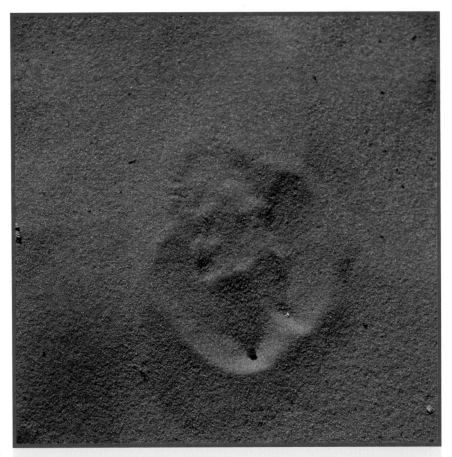

Many coyotes live in the arid environment of the desert of the southwestern United States. This coyote footprint has been left behind in the desert sands.

southern provinces of Canada to central Mexico. Most coyotes lived in the prairies, where there were many small mammals for the coyotes to eat. A few smaller coyote populations lived in the desert and semi-desert regions of the American Southwest and Mexico.

Although prairies were the coyotes' main habitat, wolves were the prairie's top predators—and coyotes were often part of the wolf's menu. Wolves occupied forests, forcing the coyotes to stay in the open spaces of the plains. The coyotes of the plains were not strong enough to kill large prey but, as scavengers, they ate what was left over after wolves killed buffalo, elk, and deer.

Chapter 2

Coyotes in Myth and Culture

Early Ideas About the Coyote

MANY NATIVE AMERICAN TRIBES tell stories about coyotes as well as other animals, such as bears and cougars. The Native Americans describe the character of each type of animal. Usually, the coyote is depicted as a trickster or troublemaker. At times, the coyote is a fool and other times a hero. Sometimes coyotes are even said to influence the gods.

Many myths describe the coyote as a wild trickster.

A Hopi story tells how the coyote got its yellow eyes. Like all folk tales, the story has changed as it has been told over many years. Here is one version:

One time, Coyote Woman was hunting and came upon a medicine man called Skeleton. She saw that when Skeleton Man would sing a song, his eyes would fly out of his head and go south until they were out of sight. Then they would return to his eye sockets.

The Coyote Woman said, "Oh, wise Skeleton Man. Would you teach me that song so that I can see what you see?"

The Skeleton Man said, "I have seen many wonderful things and I will teach you the song. Just be sure to face south and do not move."

The Skeleton Man left and the Coyote Woman sang his song. Her eyes, too, flew out of her head and went south.

A COYOTE IN OUR POPULAR CULTURE

Wile E. Coyote, a coyote, is one of the most famous American cartoon characters. This Looney Tunes and Merrie Melodies character, created by artist Chuck Jones in 1949, is best known for his constant unsuccessful pursuit of the Road Runner. The original Wile E. Coyote cartoons were based on a quotation from Mark Twain's book *Roughing It*, in which Twain says that coyotes are so hungry that they would chase anything, including a roadrunner.

But Coyote Woman's eyes did not return. In her excitement, she had turned her head and her eyes could not find their way back to her head.

She searched for her lost eyes frantically. Finally, she found two eyes on the ground and put them in her head. But when she opened her eyes, everything she saw was yellow.

MARK TWAIN WRITES ABOUT COYOTES

In his 1872 book *Roughing It,* author Mark Twain described coyotes in a very negative way. Here is an excerpt from Twain's book:

The coyote is a long, slim, sick and sorry-looking skeleton, with a gray wolfskin stretched over it, a tolerably bushy tail that forever sags down with a despairing expression of forsakenness and misery, a furtive and evil eye, and a long, sharp face, with slightly lifted lip and exposed teeth. He has a general slinking expression all over. The coyote is a living, breathing allegory of Want. He is always hungry. He is always poor, out of luck, and friendless. The meanest creatures despise him, and even the fleas would desert him for a velocipede. He is so spiritless and cowardly that even while his exposed teeth are pretending a threat, the rest of his face is apologizing for it. And he is so homely!—so scrawny, and ribby, and coarse-haired, and pitiful.

The Coyote Woman went home to her pups. When they saw her eyes, they were frightened and ran away, saying, "Oh, mama, your eyes are all yellow!"

The Coyote Woman had accidentally replaced her eyes with yellow gourds. Ever since then, she has had yellow eyes and all her children have yellow eyes, too.

As shown by this story, Native Americans—as well as fur trappers, traders, and early settlers—looked at the coyote with amusement. They saw it as a scavenger that lived by its wits. Many people could sympathize with the coyote's tricky character because they, too, had to use their wits to survive. They admired the coyote's cleverness and ability to make the best of a situation. This attitude toward coyotes still exists today in cartoons and children's books.

Although famous American writer Mark Twain described the sly coyote as in a negative but somewhat humorous way, others see the coyote's behavior as no joke. This sort of negative attitude would prove very dangerous to the coyote.

Chapter 3

Coyotes in Danger

"The Only Good Coyote Is a Dead Coyote"

ONE HUNDRED YEARS AGO, the unclaimed land of the Great Plains that supported the buffalo herds was gone. It had been replaced by cattle ranches and farms. Now, any predator that threatened farmers' livestock was considered an enemy to be removed. Large animals such as wolves, bears, and cougars were easy to kill. By the 1930s, the Great Plains wolf had been driven extinct. The next target was the last of the big predators: the coyote.

It would not have been unusual 20 to 40 years ago in western states like Oklahoma and Texas to drive past miles of fence posts, each with the carcass of a coyote hanging on it. Unfortunately, the practice still goes on today. Coyotes have been the victims of massive hunts by ranchers and other people whose goal is to destroy the coyote population entirely.

Government Encouragement

Occasionally, coyotes will kill newborn calves or lambs. Sometimes, they are responsible for heavy losses of livestock. Coyotes give birth at the same time as sheep and cattle and need to find food for their pups. As scavengers, they are initially attracted to birthing areas where they can feed on stillborn lambs or afterbirth. Naturally, sheep ranchers want to kill the offending coyotes to protect their own animals.

Under pressure from ranchers, the U.S. Congress authorized $125,000 to kill wolves in 1914, and Congress extended the killing to coyotes in 1916. In 1931, Congress passed a law that gave money to support the killing of any animal that damaged the industries of forestry, ranching, or farming. This included just about every wild animal, from mountain lions to gophers. In 1995, Congress appropriated $36 million for Animal Damage Control (ADC)—a unit of the Department of Agriculture.

COYOTES SURVIVE BOUNTIES

Many states pay cash bounties to encourage people to kill coyotes. This map of Kansas gives some idea of the pressure that was put on people to get rid of coyotes in 1946–1947, a time when the coyote population was high. Each full circle on the map represents 100 cash bounties that Kansas counties paid for coyotes killed, including pups that were killed in their dens. (Half circles represent 50 bounties and quarter circles represent 25.)

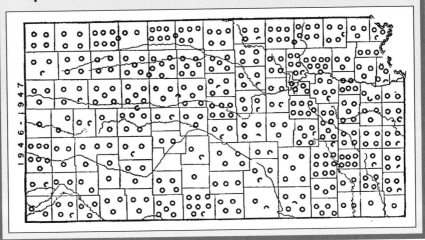

Approximately three-quarters of this money goes to protect both cattle and sheep ranchers (mostly sheep ranchers who graze their stock on both public and private lands).

Killing methods by government agents (usually local people) have included shooting, steel leg traps, cyanide cartridges, poisoned **carrion**, meatballs packed with poison and dropped by airplanes, and

Since the early years of the 20th century, the U.S. government has paid to eliminate coyotes, in an effort to protect the livestock of farmers. One of the most common methods of getting rid of coyotes is hunting.

dynamiting coyote dens. Some of these methods continue to kill and injure coyotes and many other animals.

Not everyone agrees with ADC's methods. People who are concerned about protecting wild animals generally support killing coyotes that kill sheep, but they don't support killing massive numbers of coyotes. Some people suggest that simple steps such as removing dead carcasses from the area would reduce the coyote problem for farmers and ranchers.

The real question is: How has the coyote survived decades of purposeful killing? After a mass killing, coyotes that were crafty enough to survive have several advantages. Because coyotes are sometimes predators, the number of predators is decreased and there is more food available for the surviving coyotes to eat. With a decrease in predators, mice and rabbit populations increase, especially in the spring. With this extra food, healthy, strong coyotes produce more pups per litter—sometimes as many as 12 pups. With a good food supply, more of these pups survive.

Although effective in limiting cattle and sheep losses, the effects of killing coyotes and other predators are temporary. Attempts at massive killings simply do not work. Even when 40 to 50 percent of coyotes are killed annually each year, the coyote population bounces back. The massive killings have had a devastating effect on other wildlife. When left alone, the coyote populations level off and are fairly constant.

It is important to note that coyote attacks on humans are extremely rare. There is only one recorded death from a coyote attack, which occurred to a child in California. In October 2000, in Phoenix, Arizona, a female coyote entered a house and tried to drag a 22-month-old boy outside. The boy's father scared the coyote away, and the boy was treated for bites to his shoulder. Although the risk of coyote

LIVING WITH COYOTES

These tips, from the Massachusetts Division of Fisheries and Wildlife, suggest ways to avoid problems with coyotes in suburban areas.

Secure your garbage. Coyotes raid open trash materials and compost piles. Secure your garbage in tough plastic containers with tight fitting lids and keep them in secure buildings when possible. Take out trash when the morning pickup is scheduled, not the previous night. Keep compost in secure, vented containers, and keep barbecue grills clean to reduce attractive odors.

Don't feed or try to pet coyotes. Keep wild things wild. Feeding, whether direct or indirect, can cause coyotes to act tame and may lead to bold behavior. Coyotes that rely on natural foods remain wild and wary of humans.

Signs in some areas remind people not to feed coyotes.

Keep your pets safe. Although free roaming pets are more likely to be killed by automobiles than by wild animals, coyotes do view cats and small dogs as potential food, and larger dogs as competition. For the safety of your pets, keep them indoors or on a leash at all times.

Keep bird feeder areas clean. Use feeders designed to keep seeds off the ground, since the seed attracts many small mammals coyotes prey upon. Remove feeders if coyotes are regularly seen around your yard.

Feed pets indoors. Outdoor feeding attracts many wild animals to your door.

Close off crawl spaces under porches and sheds. Coyotes use such areas for resting and raising young.

Don't let coyotes intimidate you. Don't hesitate to scare or threaten coyotes with loud noises, bright lights, or water sprayed from a hose.

Cut back brushy edges in your yard. These areas provide cover for coyotes and their prey.

Protect livestock and produce. Coyotes will prey on livestock. Various techniques, such as fencing, will protect livestock from predation. Clear fallen fruit from around fruit trees.

Source: Massachusetts Division of Fisheries and Wildlife. "Living With Wildlife: Eastern Coyotes in Massachusetts." Available online at *http://www.mass.gov/dfwele/dfw/dfwcoy.htm.*

attacks is low, young children should not be left alone where coyotes roam freely, especially in the evening when coyotes are usually hunting for food. In contrast to the very rare coyote attacks, there were 177 known dog-bite fatalities between 1979 and 1994 in the United States. Thousands of people are bitten by dogs each year.

Chapter 4

Migration and Lifestyle

What Do Coyotes Eat?

THE COYOTE DIET VARIES with the season and with what foods are available. A Kansas study of the stomach contents of coyotes over a 15-year period found that 75 percent or more of a coyote's diet consists of rabbits, hares (jackrabbits), rodents, and carrion. During the winter, these three food sources made up almost 90 percent of the coyote's diet.

When an area has many rabbits and hares, life is good for coyotes because they can easily get the 1.5 pounds

(0.68 kg) of meat they need each day to survive. In good times, a coyote does not eat all of the animals it kills, but it will kill a rabbit each day. This preference for fresh meat keeps the rabbit population under control. A single coyote may eat about 1,000 meadow mice a year when they are plentiful, thus reducing the breeding population of mice. This is helpful, since a common meadow mouse destroys 25 pounds (11.3 kg) of grass a year. Coyotes serve an important function: keeping two plant-eaters—rabbits and rodents—in check, and preserving grazing land.

THE COYOTE'S MENU

Meat: Rabbits, mice, cotton rats, ground squirrels, prairie dogs, prairie chickens, pheasants, crayfish, fawns, deer, calves, lambs, ground hogs, any dead or weakened animal, fish, crickets, grasshoppers, beetles, frogs, snakes, lizards, dead coyotes

Vegetables: Grass, melons (especially watermelons), juniper berries, various roots and bulbs, acorns, apples, cactus fruits, corn, vegetables farmers grow

Dessert: Occasional small dog or cat, especially those out at night

Miscellaneous: Garbage

Avoids (but would eat if necessary): Voles, moles, Norway rats, house mice, skunks

Coyote Migration

Before pioneers began to move to the Great Plains, coyotes lived on the tall- and short-grass prairies of the Midwest. Scattered populations of coyotes also extended east around the Great Lakes and south into Mexico. The coyotes' first big movement into new territory occurred with the Yukon gold strike of 1896. As prospectors started their trek over the Rocky Mountains to the gold fields, the coyotes followed them north into the Yukon and Alaska. Coyotes lived on garbage, dead mules, and anything else the humans left behind.

After invading Alaska, coyotes migrated east into newly created farmlands. By the early 1900s, the forests of eastern Canada and the eastern United States were largely replaced by farms, and wolves were almost eliminated, opening up more territory for coyotes. In Ontario, Canada, coyotes followed the railroad lines and roads north of Lake Superior and farther east to the northern shores of Lake Huron. They also moved east through Wisconsin and Illinois, up into Michigan, and into southern Ontario. New York, Maine, Pennsylvania, and Ohio all had reports of coyotes being sighted before 1938. Farther south, the Mississippi River was a formidable barrier for coyotes to cross. Coyotes that were imported for hunting may have been a major factor in establishing populations in the southern states.

PREDATOR-PREY RELATIONSHIPS

The number of prey is influenced by the number of predators and vice versa. Prey could be a population of herbivores, such as rabbits, ground squirrels, or field mice, while predators could be coyotes, wolves, hawks, or any number of different carnivores. Prey organisms always outnumber predators. Nobody would expect lions to outnumber gazelles on the African plains any more than anteaters could outnumber the ants they eat.

A crash in the predator population could be the result of natural causes, such as drought or disease. If the predators are coyotes, however, a crash could be caused by an "extermination hunt" in which hunters kill as many coyotes as they can find. Usually a few coyotes survive, and they start to rebuild the population. If the predator population does not rebuild, then the prey population may quickly grow out of control.

Coyotes are now widespread throughout much of North and Central America. The distribution, however, is far from uniform. Even distribution within any given state may vary widely. The opportunistic coyote has taken advantage of the drastic changes humans have caused. They have adapted to the frigid climate of Alaska, the suburbs outside of New York City, and the tropics of Central America. In fact, all U.S. states except Hawaii have coyote populations.

Coyotes are good at adapting to different environments. Some coyotes even live in the cold, icy tundras of Alaska.

Coyotes have even been spotted in New York City and in downtown Los Angeles. Perhaps it would be easier to stop trying to kill coyotes and learn how to live with them. They're clearly here to stay.

The Eastern Coyote Is Different

Science is not a simple process that always leads to agreed-upon explanations. Sometimes arguments rage for years before enough facts are gathered to bring about a consensus. A debate is currently going on about the eastern coyote.

The eastern coyote's average weight is 20 to 30 percent higher than that of the western coyote, with some males reaching more than 50 pounds (23 kg). They're larger and have bigger heads. Eastern coyote packs are larger, with three to seven or even more members. Eastern coyotes hunt larger game, such as white-tailed deer. All of these traits are more like those of wolves than western coyotes. What factors made the eastern coyote more wolf-like?

One view is that gray wolves mated with coyotes to produce coyote **hybrids** that had wolf-like characteristics. However, there are also other possible reasons. The changes may have occurred in response to the new environment. Coyotes had adapted well to living in the prairies and deserts of the western United States and now found themselves in a very different place. They could no longer depend on small animals as their main source of food. The new food supply—mainly deer and snowshoe hares—in the eastern forests was a strong factor in making the coyotes larger and encouraging them to form larger packs. For a pack of coyotes, bringing down a deer is dangerous. The strongest, largest coyotes were the most successful at it. Over time, these animals reproduced at a faster rate than the smaller, weaker coyotes. Slowly, due to the pressure of natural selection, eastern coyotes changed to take on wolf-like characteristics. In a sense, the eastern coyotes have filled an

The eastern coyote is larger than its western counterpart, perhaps because the prey it hunts in eastern forests, such as deer, are larger than what coyotes hunt elsewhere.

empty niche—a way of life—that was once occupied by wolves.

One other view is that coyotes may have mated with domestic dogs, such as Labradors or German shepherds, and produced large hybrids called **coydogs**. Coydogs do exist, but many biologists consider them insignificant—just a "blip" in the story of coyotes and their evolution.

Chapter 5

Coyote Family Life

Pack Formation

COYOTES WERE SHAPED BY a prairie environment where they learned to hunt smaller animals and scavenge the remains left behind by more dominant predators such as the wolf, bear, and cougar. Feeding on small prairie animals leads coyotes to be small in size and to maintain small family units of two or sometimes three, the third member being a young coyote.

The mated pair is the basic social unit. The size of the family is determined by the availability of food. For

A mated pair dominates a pack of coyotes, which may include around four to seven coyotes.

example, a pack of four to seven coyotes may form when siblings stay with the family through the winter to help defend the food supply. Feeding together and defending food supplies help strengthen the bonds between family members and decrease the rivalry between siblings. However, siblings rarely stay together longer than one year. Another factor that causes pack formation is a lack of territory and mates for the young coyotes. A mated pair always dominates the pack, no matter how big it is.

Sometimes young coyotes that have just left the family or have survived their first winter form temporary groups with other unattached coyotes. These groups can range in size from about 7 to 20 coyotes. Groups make hunting easier. These temporary groups, called **aggregates**, have no leaders or family structure, and individual coyotes leave the group after a short time.

People walking dogs have occasionally found themselves being studied from a distance by a pack of coyotes. After a short time, the coyotes lose interest and run off. Although this can make people uncomfortable and even frightened, biologists generally agree that the dog—not the owner—was the center of attraction for the coyotes.

Mating Rituals

A young female coyote that has just left her family unit and is hunting alone in winter has a difficult time surviving. Under such conditions, bonding between male and female can benefit both coyotes.

Coyotes make their presence known by howling. If a male is in the area and hears a howl from a female, he may seek out the newcomer. Most likely, the two will meet while they are hunting. When they do meet, the female may ignore the male at first. After four or five meetings, she may accept the male as a hunting partner, in which case there will be some nose touching and a lot of tail wagging. The two coyotes hunt together but sleep separately.

Coyotes only attempt to mate in the early spring. If mating occurs, the bonding of the two coyotes becomes permanent. They are mated for life. Their devotion to one another is an important factor in their ability not only to survive but to flourish in an extremely hostile environment.

Raising a Family

In the spring, the mated pair of coyotes searches for a den. They may choose a new den, but they often return to a den they have used before. The den is usually an enlarged area at the end of a tunnel. Some tunnels are dug straight into a bank, and then enlarged. Others may go down about 2 to 3 feet (0.6 to 0.9 m) and then level off. The length of the tunnel depends on the difficulty of digging. Some are only 5 to 6 feet (1.5 to 1.8 m) long, others may be up to 15 to 30 feet (4.6 to 9.1 m) long, and some have side chambers.

The den is chosen by the female and may be located in an abandoned dump, a ravine covered with heavy brush, under a shed, or on the side of a cliff— a place as safe from humans as possible. In a city, the female may have her pups under a pile of wood or in an abandoned building. Coyotes adapt to their environment. Sometimes, they prepare more than one den site. That way, if their pups are discovered, they can be moved to the new site.

Coyotes build their dens in tunnels dug into the soil, often near a tree or other shelter.

Female coyotes are pregnant for a period of 60 to 63 days and typically give birth to 3 to 9 pups (sometimes more), depending on the health of the mother and the availability of food. The pups are born hairless and blind. The nursing mother is fed by her mate and, in some cases, by a one-year-old helper. They sometimes bring food directly from the kill or **regurgitate** meat eaten at the site of the kill. After five days, the mother leaves the den and returns from hunting to nurse her pups.

If no other shelter is available, coyotes may build their dens in abandoned dumps or other human-made sites.

Puppy Life

The pups open their eyes in about 10 days. In about three weeks, they venture out of the den. At first, the mother "baby-sits" the pups. A short, distant howl from one of the adult coyotes will send the mother and her pups scurrying back into the den.

Outside the den, nursing takes place four times a day and is usually done with the mother standing while the pups stand on their hind legs to get milk.

This position lets the mother watch for danger and also strengthens the hind legs of the pups.

The pups investigate everything in sight. As with many mammals, play introduces pups to skills they need to survive. A tug-of-war over part of a rabbit or a live mouse introduces the puppies to the taste of blood, meat, and bone. During this time, the mother may go hunting while one of the other adults stands guard.

As the pups grow teeth, nursing becomes painful for the mother. She begins to wean her pups gradually in the fifth to seventh week after they are born. As the mother lengthens the time between feedings, the pups gradually adapt to eating the regurgitated food brought in by the adults instead of their mother's milk.

GAMES THAT HELP COYOTES TRAIN TO HUNT

Coyotes love to play, and playing helps them prepare for the hard work of hunting. In keeping with its reputation as a trickster, a coyote will sometimes get a dog to chase it, knowing that it can easily outrun the dog. The coyote will stay in front just enough to lead the dog on. When the dog slows, the coyote slows. Then, when the dog is exhausted, the coyote will put on a burst of speed, leaving the dog far behind. The coyote will stop and turn to watch the hot, exhausted, thirsty dog turn to walk a long way back home.

Although pups and juveniles are guarded by the adults, they may be swept up by a hawk or taken by a bobcat or other predator at any moment. Worst of all, their den may be discovered by ranchers who will often dig out the coyotes and kill them. If one pup is taken by a predator, the adult coyotes will show some confusion and anxiety at first but will very quickly resume normal activity. This is not to suggest that coyotes cannot feel loss. They may simply be unable to count.

Life as a Juvenile

One scientific study showed that in some years the mortality rate for coyotes less than one year old was as high as 60 to 70 percent. Hunting, trapping, starvation, predators, disease, and the cold of winter take a high toll. If the coyotes survive the first year, however, their chances of having a normal life span increase greatly. A coyote living in the wild has an average life span of about nine years.

Another study conducted with small radio transmitters inserted into the body cavities of young coyotes found that one had traveled over 100 miles (161 km) after leaving its parents. This helps explain the coyotes' migration into new territories that had previously been cleared of coyotes.

The lessons learned at the den and the puppies' rapid growth prepare them for hunting. The training is tough and always full of danger. In one study, more than half of the coyote pups died of diseases, parasites, or starvation, or were killed by predators (including humans) within seven months.

The juveniles learn that a wide variety of foods, including insects and fruits, can also be part of their diet. They watch adults hunt and learn that cooperation between adults increases the chances of success. Competition between siblings increases with time, and the more aggressive juveniles may fight off other siblings for the best pieces of meat. A pecking order forms; if food is scarce, less aggressive pups may starve.

Sleeping at night often takes place outside rather than in the den. As the pups grow up, they become more independent and start to wander farther away from the group.

Learning About the Environment

As coyotes mature, they continually learn about their environment. For example, coyotes have to learn to avoid poisonous snakes, especially in the desert. It takes only one or two encounters at a young age for the coyote to learn to fear snakes. The pup has to learn how to respond when a sudden shadow is cast by a hawk or eagle overhead. It has to learn how to stay still to avoid detection when a bobcat is near. A pup's schooling period usually lasts only a few months before it has to survive on its own in a very hostile environment.

Learning About Territorial Boundaries

Humans stake out individual territories that are recognized by others. Coyotes, too, have territories that help ensure their survival. Juvenile coyotes have to learn the boundaries of their territory, which may vary from a few square miles to 30 square miles (77.7 square km). Boundaries may be an old road, a fence line, a deep ditch, or a line of trees on a hill. Sometimes the boundary lines are unmarked. If a juvenile or adult unknowingly trespasses on another coyote's territory, it could be killed.

Yearlings who have survived a winter, and older unattached coyotes, wander the countryside looking for a mate and a territory to claim. Once a mate is found and a territory is claimed, the coyotes have to protect their claim's boundaries. After the first litter is born, the family unit (the parents and usually one yearling), defends the territory. Usually a bark, growl, or some display of threat will discourage an invader. Sometimes, however, the invading coyote is attacked or even killed.

The Aggregate, a Social Group

Juveniles usually leave their family units or are driven off in the fall or winter. These include the juveniles less than one year old as well as the yearlings that helped raise that year's pups. Striking out on their own and finding food during the winter is difficult. They must avoid not only predators but also trespassing on another coyote family's territory, which could result in death or serious injury.

In densely populated areas, these migrating juveniles may meet and form very loose social groups called aggregates. These groups may also include mated pairs and older individuals. Aggregates often meet where food, including carrion, is available. They are more likely to form during the winter in regions such as river valleys or around large lakes.

Compared to packs, aggregates lack the social structure and order that the dominance by a mating pair and maintaining a certain territory bring. Aggregates do, however, offer advantages. They help protect members from predators, guard supplies of food, and pursue larger game. Wild domestic dogs also form aggregates.

The Single Coyote

A single coyote will sometimes make a den and hunt within certain boundaries. Single coyotes can also be constant travelers. These solo coyotes do not defend their territory against intruders.

Single coyotes include young and mature healthy adults as well as some injured coyotes. They simply

Although most coyotes travel in small packs, a single coyote will sometimes live and hunt on its own.

wander over a broad area in search of food. Some travel more than 200 miles (322 km) in a single year. In one study of coyotes in southeastern Colorado, 22 percent were constant travelers.

Chapter 6

Hunting

Hunting Techniques

SEARCH AND POUNCE is one of the first techniques a young coyote masters. It's important in capturing the small game that make up a lot of the coyote's diet.

In the spiral technique, the female coyote takes a concealed position in a depression behind a log or brush, and waits. The male scares up a jackrabbit and proceeds to chase it. A rabbit can often outrun a coyote, but in this case, the pursuing coyote stays slightly to one side of the

One of the most common methods of hunting is to search for small prey and then pounce on it.

rabbit so that it runs a little to the other side in what becomes a spiral that leads toward the hidden female. If a juvenile coyote is present, it may take over the chase if the male gets tired. Eventually, the spiral closes, and the rabbit comes within range of the waiting female, who attacks. All of the coyotes that took part in the hunt share in the meal.

Coyotes are opportunists. This can be seen in the relationship that has evolved between the badger and the coyote. When a coyote sees a badger on the hunt for ground squirrels, it tags along at a safe distance. When the badger starts to dig out the squirrels, the coyote will scurry around looking for exit holes. When the squirrels panic and rush out of their burrows to escape the badger, the coyote pounces on them. With any luck, it can get several meals. Apache and Navaho Indians referred to the coyote and badger as "cousins." Early pioneers also wrote about this partnership.

With the increasing coyote population, ravens are becoming more plentiful in the northeastern forests. The relationship between ravens and wolves is well documented, but it may apply to ravens and coyotes as well. Experts believe that in the winter, ravens direct coyotes to prey by flying around and cawing. Hunting in snow, especially deep snow, requires a lot of energy. Coyotes save their energy by responding to the raven calls to help them find prey. In return, the ravens, which are unable to kill their own prey, scavenge what is left over after the coyote's meal.

To a coyote with several pups to feed, a small dog is an easy meal. The coyote studies the habits of humans and knows that the dog will be let out at a certain time. It waits patiently. As soon as the dog is within range, the coyote charges in and grabs the dog, usually around the neck, killing it instantly. Sometimes the dog does not even have time to yelp. The coyote and the dog disappear in a flash. Upset owners often report that they saw only a

Some coyotes live in suburbs and other areas close to humans.

COYOTES LIVING AMONG US

There have been only a few studies of the coyotes that survive in the suburbs. In 1976, a male yearling coyote that had been living in suburban Lincoln, Nebraska, was captured. A radio transmitter collar was attached to the animal's neck, and its movements were tracked 24 hours a day for 63 days between April and July. The coyote's home range covered about 4.6 square miles (11.9 square km).

The coyote was most active from midnight to 6:00 A.M. and from 5:30 P.M. to 9:30 P.M. About 70 percent of its activity took place in a small suburban area of about 35 acres (14 hectares) where food and shelter were available. To get to this area, the coyote had to cross streets and run between houses. Although it took care to avoid humans, the coyote was observed by residents on 44 days of the 65-day study. The coyote was much more daring at night, approaching to within 30 meters (32.8 yards) of a woman walking her dog.

Coyotes live in areas all across North America. They live in all kinds of terrain, from desert to tundra to suburb.

shadow flash past and did not realize for a while what happened.

Coyotes Are Both Predators and Prey

Just two years after wolves were reintroduced in Yellowstone National Park in 1995 through 1996, the coyote population was cut in half. Wolves kill coyotes, and it did not take long for wolves to go back to their old pre-pioneer role as top predator in the region.

A similar situation happens when coyotes invade the territory of the red fox. Coyotes kill foxes that compete with them for food. Coyotes are now the top predators in the area around the city of Boulder, Colorado. The foxes that once lived in this region have moved into the outermost suburbs of Boulder in order to survive. Evidently, the foxes' fear of coyotes is stronger than their fear of humans, and they have learned how to live closer to humans. It is not unusual to have a family of foxes living very close to suburban homes due to their fear of being killed by coyotes.

Chapter 7

Coyote Communication

The Howl

THE BEST-KNOWN COYOTE trait is its howl, and most people remember the first time they hear it. If you're with other people or in a safe environment, hearing a coyote howl can be an enjoyable experience. If you're alone in the wilderness, however, it can be upsetting and even scary.

Howling can begin with a lone coyote. The howl is long, loud, and rather high-pitched with a wavering

Hearing the sound of a coyote's howl is an unforgettable experience.

sound that is beautiful to hear. When one coyote starts howling, other members of the group join in. It is a greeting and may serve to call the family together for the evening hunt. The group howl is a way to strengthen bonding within the group and for coyotes to announce their presence to other groups. Each coyote's howl is unique and defines the individual. Family members can tell one another apart from members of other groups just by the sound of their howls. Aside from communication, coyotes probably howl at times just for the joy of it.

The Group Yip-Howl

Sometimes, a different sound—the group bark, or yip-howl—is made. The yipping is a high-pitched bark followed by a howl. It, too, can be a greeting to members of the same group, but it is more often a strong show of territory. The yip-howl is answered, and several family groups join in, each announcing its presence. Soon the yipping, barking, and howling are a major event. It seems as if each group wants to "out-howl" the others.

These sounds are usually heard in the evening. They are a way for all coyote family groups in the region to announce their territory; and it may help prevent visual contact between groups when they are hunting. Group howls signal how many coyotes are in a region and may encourage juveniles either to run away or stay together. It also lets coyotes know which territories are open.

Group howls may go on for 15 to 20 minutes. Hearing them is an unforgettable experience. As more coyotes join in the chorus, they vary their pitch and increase the number of yips. They have a great time!

aggregates—Temporary groups of coyotes, most of which are either young or unattached.

canids—Meat-eating animals that include coyotes, domesticated dogs, wolves, jackals, and foxes.

carrion—The dead body of an animal.

coydog—A cross between a coyote and a domesticated dog.

evolution—Process by which animals develop into new species by adapting their traits to better fit into their environments.

food chain—A hierarchy of living things within the same habitat. At the top are predators, in the middle are the prey of these predators, and at bottom are the plants and insects that both the prey and predators eat.

hybrid—The offspring of two animals of different species.

muzzle—The snout of an animal; the nose and jaws.

natural selection—A process by which those animals that are best adapted to their environment survive to reproduce.

regurgitate—Bring partly digested food back up from the stomach.

scavengers—Animals that feed on dead animals.

Andelt, W. F., and B. R. Mahan. "Behavior of an Urban Coyote." *The American Midland Naturalist* 103 (1980): 399–400.

Bekoff, Max. "Coyotes: Victims of Their Own Success." *Canid News* 3(1995).

Gier, H. T. "Coyotes in Kansas." *Kansas State Agricultural Experimental Station Bulletin* 393 (1968): 68.

Harrison, Daniel J. *Social Ecology of Coyotes in Northeastern North America: Relationships to Dispersal, Food Resources, and Exploitation.* Orono, ME: Department of Wildlife, University of Maine, Fredericson, D. Wildlife Research Unit, University of New Brunswick, 1992, pp. 53–72.

Lehner, Philip N. "Coyote Vocalizations: A Lexicon and Comparisons With Other Canids." *Animal Behavior* 26 (1978): 712–722.

Litvaitis, John A. *Niche Relations Between Coyotes and Sympatric Carnivora.* Durham, NH: Department of Natural Resources, University of New Hampshire, Fredericson, D., Wildlife Research Unit, University of New Brunswick, 1992, pp. 73–77.

Moore, Gary C., and Garry R. Parker. "Colonization of the Eastern Coyote (*Canis latrans*)." *Coyote*, ed. Arnold H. Boer. Wildlife Research Unit, University of New Brunswick, 1992, pp. 23–37.

Wayne, Robert K., and Niles Lehman. "Mitochondrial DNA Analysis of the Eastern Coyote: Origins and Hybridization." *Coyote*, ed. Arnold H. Boer. Wildlife Research Unit, University of New Brunswick, 1992, pp. 9–21.

Bekoff, Mark, ed. *Coyotes: Biology, Behavior and Management.* Caldwell, NJ: Blackburn Press, 2001.

Reid, Catherine. *Coyote: Seeking the Hunter in Our Midst.* Boston: Houghton Mifflin, 2004.

Trout, John, Jr. *Solving Coyote Problems: How to Coexist with North America's Most Persistent Predator.* Guilford, CT: The Lyons Press, 2001.

Yule, Lauray. *Coyotes.* Tucson, AZ: Rio Nuevo Publishers, 2004.

Web Sites

"Coyotes." National Geographic for Kids. *www.nationalgeographic.com/kids/ creature_feature/0005/coyote.html.*

"Coyotes." Yellowstone National Park. *www.nps.gov/yell/nature/animals/ Coyote/coyote.html.*

Predator Defense Institute *www.predatordefense.org*

Wildlife Services *www.aphis.usda.gov/ws*

PICTURE CREDITS

ABOUT THE AUTHOR

James V. Bradley taught biology at Lake Forest High School in Lake Forest, Illinois, for 25 years. He also taught science in Colorado and in the United Kingdom. Bradley received the Illinois STAR Award (Science Teaching Achievement Recognition) in 1980 and was named by the National Association of Biology Teachers as outstanding biology teacher in Illinois in 1981. He retired from teaching in 1994, but continues to write and study science topics.